SIKE WARD

BY MEGAN FOLEY

Sike Ward

Books may be purchased in quantity and/or special sales by contacting the publisher. All inquiries related to such matters should be addressed to:

South Broadway Press LLC
1350 Josephine St, Unit 102
Denver CO 80206

southbroadwaypress@gmail.com

303.330.8083

First Paperback Edition, 2026
ISBN: 978-1-7350355-7-4
Library of Congress Control Number: 9781735035574

Cover Art: "Soft Tissue" by Ally Ducey
Cover Design: Brice Maiurro

Printed in the United States

PRAISE FOR SIKE WARD

"I've had the shit kicked out of me more gently than this..."

—JORDAN WYBERNEIT

"Strange, deranged, and joyful..."

—DEBRA KEANE, EDITOR, SOUTH BROADWAY PRESS

"[Sike Ward] shows the importance of living, even when it's the hardest thing in the world.

—MAPLE SCORESBY

"With formal experimentation, dark humor, and deep queer caring, Foley's poems are ornate chandeliers beaming with light and promise to crush."

—AERIK FRANCIS, ADAMS COUNTY POET LAUREATE

TABLE OF CONTENTS

SIKE WARD

Megan Foley

SOUTH BROADWAY PRESS
DENVER CO USA

Dear Reader,

This work contains dark themes and heavy topics. It includes: frank discussions of mental health, violence, death, and suicide. This is not appropriate for all readers, and individual discretion is advised. I ask that you please take care of yourself. If this book is not for you, I hope you put it down and have a great time doing something else. But if this is for you, I hope it hits like a truck. I hope it floats in the wreckage and helps carry you through. I write about this darkness because I need to, but also because I know others need to hear it too. May it give you hope.

Suicide Hotline Number: 988

For those who kept me alive;
may we all be taken in the Poet Rapture.

"Mom, what's more punk rock
than living despite all that
which has tried to make you not?"

—Neil Hilborn

Joy Wizard the Wizard of Joy

My therapist has a doctorate in Joy Wizard summoning.

From my spot on the couch I can count the fancy frames on the far wall. Her office breathes a little louder whenever we talk about him.

"So you haven't seen him?"

"No." I stir my coffee—maybe a tad too aggressively. I wonder if I'm expected to elaborate. If she wants me to say out loud that I have been forsaken by the Wizard of Joy. Do I have to admit I can't quite lift my own body weight out of bed? Do you think she can tell just by looking at me that my happiness machine broke? I used to be the underweight champion of the world; depression got hoisted up onto my shoulders and carried for miles.

No.

No, there is no Joy Wizard in my coffee. He doesn't show up to my volleyball games. I haven't run into him at the store, or the park, or the library, or at any of my friends' houses, or the doctor's office, or my bathroom floor, or the on-ramp of I-80. He is absent from all the hundreds of selfies I take and delete. I only vaguely remember what he looks like.

The Wizard of Joy has gone to ground. And my therapist says I shouldn't envision myself a starving work hound—but if I can't drag him from his burrow, can't get my teeth around the Joy Wizard's bloody ankle and pull, then how am I expected to get him back? Who else will count my ribs while lecturing me on patience?

I stand still for too long in the dim parking lot of my therapist's office.

"What did I do?" I kick a rock off the pavement and into the gutter. "What did I do to earn the ire of the Wizard of Joy?"

And he appears.

Standing beside me in the dark—as if to prove that the Joy Wizard knew what ire meant—is the Wizard of Joy.

"Y'know," he says, and leans back against the hood of my car. He never smiles at me. "Sometimes when healing, we don't even start to break until we feel safe enough."

And then he's gone again.

Depression Monster Reprise

Depression Monster kidnaps me in broad daylight
Depression Monster holds my mother's hand while she cries
Depression Monster helps put up missing posters
Depression Monster wears my skin

When my name is called in the waiting room
Depression Monster jumps up to follow me back
Dr. *Have-You-Tried-Yoga* reads the black box warning
Depression Monster is taking notes

When the insurance rep calls
Depression Monster picks up the phone
Depression Monster bows his head in prayer
Depression Monster leaves me tied up in his basement

Depression Monster takes my body for a spin
Depression Monsters goes to concerts and theme parks
Depression Monster takes selfies that are proof of life
Depression Monster eats the last of my peanut butter

Depression Monster never goes away, really
The way that, when you are driving into the sunrise
It can be morning almost forever

SURVIVAL EXHIBIT 07

I Talked to My Doctor About My New and Worsening Thoughts of Suicide and All I Got Was This Stupid Bill

I sleep in the bed
of the girl who tries to kill me

I wear her clothes
I drive her car

I take her Lithium pills
and vitamin B supplements

I hold her hair
when she pukes

I hold her hand
when the bear of Depression

sits on her chest
rips

strips
of meat and muscle

she is being eaten alive
and I cannot help her

I cannot kill her
her mother would never forgive me

I drag her into the bathroom
to make her brush our teeth

we lock eyes in the mirror
"Are you going to kill me?"

"No.
I'm going to wash your face."

I lie in bed wanting to die
and smelling of coconut

SURVIVAL EXHIBIT 270

Compression Artifact

I scroll through your screenshots while you're in the shower.

On the whole, they're completely unsurprising. Things you want to remember, kept in a place you've already forgotten: recipes, restaurants. That wine-&-painting place we wanted to go to that was replaced by an urgent care last year. Top ten books to read if you want to start shadow work. Pictures of corgi puppies wearing cowboy boots.

I open another folder and stop when a headline catches my eye: *"Why the World Bank is on the brink of great disaster."*[1]

The next one is a headline, too: *"Close up video shows Texas floating barrier has circular saws."*[2]

Then a cascade of screenshots: *"A mom owed nearly $100,000 for her son's stay in a state mental hospital."*[3] *"When politicians have no shame, the old rules don't apply."*[4] *"How to get approved for a $5,000 p*ndemic loan after being DENIED."*[5] *"Don't buy evil chocolate."*[6] *"This July 4th, today's youth are unprepared to win a revolutionary war."*[7] *"Food is getting cheaper, but not for you."*[8] *"AI tasked with destroying humanity now trying new tactic."*[9] *"The end of world order as we know it."*[10]

I open the next folder, hoping to go back to pictures of dogs. Instead, I am met with everything you saved about the last election. It's been months, but here in this dark little corner of your phone you have enshrined a play-by-play of every excruciating detail. A swarm of two-toned graphs that overtake everything else. Screenshot after screenshot of a little red and blue map, the number at the top changing with each slide.

I'm swiping past as fast as I can now. The scrolling images pass in a dizzying stop-motion animation. A zoetrope of the numbers slowly ticking down. The decision unfilling the map. Time winding back and the information disappearing. The last one is completely gray—a blank map showing nothing.

I put your phone down. I never say anything about it. You never delete the pictures.

[1-10] *See Works Cited for complete list of media referenced*

Behold! The World's Slowest Drowning Woman

It takes a long time to fill a studio apartment with water
The record number of days spent adrift at sea is 438
Set by career sailors in a small fiberglass fishing boat
There were two of them, at first
Drinking blood directly from the necks of seabirds
After four months one lost hope and refused to eat
After six days of talking to a corpse
The survivor dumped his friend's body into the ocean

It takes a long time to fill a studio apartment with water
One woman, after her plane went down
Spent 11 days trekking through the coastal jungle
The headlines called it a case of "textbook survival"
Within 3 months, she flew back home and returned to her job
She has worked hard to forget the smells

It takes a long time to fill a studio apartment with water
It takes 38 pounds of pressure to crush a windpipe
Once, when a tugboat capsized in the Atlantic Ocean
The cook spent 3 days at the bottom of the ocean
Saved by a pocket of air trapped in the main cabin
When salvage divers came to retrieve the bodies
They found him still alive
It took 60 hours and a diving bell
To get him back to the surface

It takes a long time to fill a studio apartment with water
By the time she calls the crisis line
She has been submerged for years

The voice on the other end says, "Just tell us.
If the water closes up over your head,

All you have to do

Is say the word."

SURVIVAL EXHIBIT 3

Her Dead Name

I asked her to walk me home. Her laugh sounds like maybe I do have a future and every year for my birthday she bakes me lavender cupcakes. I knew I loved her the very moment I saw her. Now, she holds my hand and swings it gently while we walk home together.

A truck nearly hits us—one of those double-wide monstrosities with extra wheels. It goes whipping by, so close that I smell cigarette smoke through the open windows. The wind of its wake pulls at her hair, lifting the loose ends of my scarf and snapping them taut. I put a hand up. My first instinct was to make some vulgar gesture towards the driver, but she catches my arm and drags me away from the road. We stumble through a patch of long crabgrass at the edge of the sidewalk and catch our breath.

The truck stops.

Abruptly, with such force that the brakes let out a high-pitched whining noise, it comes to a halt. Its heavy frame rocking over the front wheels before it sways back to a standstill. A car swerves into the turn lane to avoid it, horn blaring as it whips by.

She's seen that truck before. I'm watching her scan the license plate and I catch the exact moment she recognizes it.

She grabs me and says, "I'm not gonna make it."

I pull away from the tremor in her voice, twisting in her grip. She's dug her long nails into the soft skin of my wrist. She holds on tight. I've never heard her sound like that.

"I won't survive," she says.

Before I can think of any kind of response, the driver's side door pops open and a man gets out. His face is concealed behind the mirrored visor of a biker helmet. I'm watching my own hazy reflection ripple as he comes towards us.

I put my body in front of hers. I remember last spring when we were camping and thought we saw a coyote on the trail; how she put herself between me and the threat. Ready to take on an entire pack armed only with a biodegradable camping spork.

The coyote was just an off-leash German Shepherd. His name was Sprinkles and he sat obediently at my feet begging for me to scratch his ears. I have a keychain can of pepper spray shoved into the side pocket of my backpack. She's still got her nails dug into my wrist.

More helmeted figures exit the truck and I am beginning to suspect that neither of us will survive. They take her from me. Her nails scratch five angry strips along my skin.

Of the four total attackers it takes three to pull her away, and only one to incapacitate me. The man who comes at me doesn't have a weapon, but it doesn't matter. The first thing he does is smash the front of his helmet into my nose. The whole faceplate comes away smeared with blood, my reflection wide-eyed and tinted red. Everything after that is choppy.

My bag goes to the ground, then so do I. His boot cracks against my jaw and I spit a trio of shattered teeth onto the sidewalk. The others are hauling her away, half-dragging, half-carrying her flailing body. After one particularly violent spasm they drop her. I hear the squelch it makes when she hits the pavement.

After that she stops fighting. They pull her, unmoving, into the truck and the doors slam. The man kicks his boot against my ribs. Then my head. I'm still trying to get up when he slams his knee into my chin. I scream. Another shard of broken tooth lands in the crabgrass. My jaw never closes the same way after that. Then the last door thumps shut and she is gone. The truck goes screaming down the road and she is gone.

I get up and fall right back down again. I get up again. I get up, get up, get up, GET UP! I get all the way through a four-lane intersection without even looking. Without even thinking about where I am running until I'm over the rocky median and I can see home on the top of the hill. I barely hear the car horns. My whole head rumbles with the sound of an idling truck.

I burst through the front door, frantic and bleeding and crying, all in that order.

You are sitting on the living room couch doing something on your phone. Your whole face goes pale at the sight of me.

I cannot get a word out. She won't survive. I don't think I will, either.

You are gentle. You hold me still to look over the wounds, but even in your careful grasp I pull away. When you grab my head in your hands my mouth falls open; a glob of blood and a bit of gum tissue dribbles out into your palm.

Finally, I think to pull up my sleeve and show you where her nails dug long red marks across my arms. Small flecks of her signature nail polish still clinging to my skin.

You take one look and call 911.

When I reach for my own phone, I find only panic. By now it's a crushed square of glass, abandoned with my backpack on the side of the road.

I scream.

The words are near unintelligible through the state of my busted face but it doesn't matter. I scream.

You have to hold me down just to talk to the first responder. Half-hug and half-restraint on the living room carpet that I'm ruining with my blood.

When you say her name, I surge up from the floor and bite you. Latch my ruined jaw onto your arm, remaining teeth sinking into the tender skin of your wrist. You don't even hit me for it—just get torn apart, bleeding into my mouth and you don't even have the decency to scream. You remain very fucking calm—repeating our address to the dispatcher like a mantra.

I asked her to walk me home.

You never give up on me. You take me to every doctor we can afford, and then a few we can't. The white-coats never reach a consensus on if my muteness is due to physical damage to my jaw or if it's psychosomatic. The scar from my bite, missing teeth and all, is faintly visible on your skin for years to come.

SURVIVAL EXHIBIT 12

How to Starve

In the three month wait between
referral and my appointment with a specialist,
you make me take up jogging.

You curate a playlist of songs that
run between 120 and 150 BPM.
The sad indie shit goes in a lock-box.

We lie lazy in the warm grass.
This is everything the doctor ordered.
and it is doing nothing.

"What would make you feel better?"

I can't tell you that it is two different things—
to not have cravings
and to be craving nothing

I say nothing.

"Tell me, honey.
That special chocolate from the store downtown?
We could order pizza tonight? Or Italian? Indian?"

I say nothing.

"I could take tomorrow off if you want.
Go drive somewhere?
Or just watch movies?"

I say nothing.

"Anything." And I've made you cry again.
"Anything, anything you need you just tell me.
I'll do it for you. Anything at all.

What do you want?"

The only thing I say
for years
is *nothing*

Lobotomy Horse As Metaphor

So in the game, if you glitch out a horse it comes back *wrong*. It loses everything that makes it a horse. The player can't interact with it using the usual prompts. There is no way to ride it or feed it or brush its tail. Whatever equipment it was carrying has now also glitched. This changes how the physics engine interacts with the used-to-be horse: it now behaves like an object.

Speed runners have nicknamed the exploit "Lobotomy Horse" and so far, have used it to shave nearly seven minutes off the world record speedrun time.

So in the game, Lobotomy Horse cannot get a job or go shopping or watch movies or get married. Not that anyone would want to marry a lobotomized horse anyhow. Lobotomy Horse always gets the bad ending. It is easy to break Lobotomy Horse. The developers never intended for Lobotomy Horse to feel joy. It gets treated like an object and so it behaves like an object. Lobotomy Horse has lost its power of attorney privileges. It can never be an animal again; there has been something fundamentally altered in its code.

Speed runners have harnessed Lobotomy Horse to clip into the basement level of the castle. This bypasses the final boss fight and beats the game in under 12 minutes. And there, in the end credits, stands Lobotomy Horse while the white text rolls over it. Try again? Will you try again?

Try again?
Try again?
Try again?

Try again?

                Try again?

                                Try   again?

Try again?

                                        Try again?

                Try again?

                        Try again?

                                Try again?

        Try again?

Try again?

Try again?

Try again?

                        Try again?

Try again?   Try again?

        Try again?   Try again?   Try again?

Try again? Try again?

                                Try again?

SURVIVAL EXHIBIT 54,550,001

NPO[1]

Do you wanna talk about it?
voice basket / empty / void
of words / I do / I can't
physically / a switch
depressed / pressed down
I can't / get the answer / out
but I want / you to love / me /
even when I don't / say the word
can't say / a word
even when I am so sick / I can't open my mouth

"I love…"
sounds / torturous
pick up / my face from the carpet
"I love   the taste   of ash"

[1] *"NPO means 'nothing by mouth,' from the Latin nil per os. The acronym is simply a doctor's shorthand for a period of time in which you may not eat or drink anything. NPO is a safety precaution." (UVA Health)*

SURVIVAL EXHIBIT 98.6
Paradoxical Undressing

I'm sorry you watched me have a panic attack
I hope you still think I'm sexy

I'm sorry I was just so happy to be here
that I didn't count my drinks

I'm sorry you made me eggs in the morning
and I barely touched them

I'm sorry anytime I cannot speak
I only clutch at your hand

I would love you to death
If you'd let me

SURVIVAL EXHIBIT 5150
Grace Period Not Covered

The envelope barely fits into the small gray mailbox. When I turn the key it pounces onto the concrete and uncurls like the legs of a dead spider. It's a packet from my insurance company—219 pages of the tiniest font I have ever seen. My coverage. My benefits. My claims. I sleep with it under my pillow. I keep it in my glovebox. When Officer *What-Are-You-Crying-For* asks for my registration, I hand him 219 pages of medical history. I can't believe I am alive. I buy an exacto knife. With surgical precision I remove every instance of the phrase "not covered."

I am the saddest little emo in the waiting room. I am having a cry in the doctor's office stairwell. Nurse *What-Brings-You-In-Today* presses a fist into my abdomen. Pushes down. Asks if there's any chance I could be pregnant. Asks if it hurts. Dr. *Sometimes-the-Self-is-Stored-in-the-Stomach* puts his hands on me. A slow-motion Heimlich maneuver. A botched stomach pump. A repeat visit. A rerun of the same episode that's always on in the background in which I play the oddest unemployed technically-adult on the parchment covered exam table. In my bed I practice counting backwards from ten. I pray to die in my sleep but still flinch when the IV goes in. I sweettalk the receptionist so she will remember my face. Unlike me, she is always a she. She tells me about her kids. If she sees that I am crying she says nothing. Dr. *Good-News-Your-Labs-Are-Normal* calls a week later.

I Google how to sign a DNR.

I make "not covered" confetti, thousands of strips of tiny paper, and glue them all to my mirror. I mail my insurance company a photo: my brother and I, 8 and 10, running down the beach.

SURVIVAL EXHIBIT 9,000

Would you love me if I were exploding?

And I mean *violently—*
the way they won't show on the news,
don't show in movies,
can't show in video games,
because it takes too much of a toll on the physics engine
to render that many tiny flying pieces.
If I never stop sounding
like a phone call in the middle of the night,
would you still love me?
Would you still love me
if I have no future
skills, and I ate all your leftovers?
Would you still love me
if I let hope walk home alone,
and that was the last anyone ever saw of her?
Would you forgive me
if I was the last one to see her alive?
If my brain were wired like a time bomb,
would you cut me in half?
Would you still love me?
And if you love me,
wouldn't you want me
to die
with a smile?

SURVIVAL EXHIBIT 76,339

Follow-up Appointment

Please-Put-Me-Out-Of-My-Misery doesn't cry during the appointment.

They make small talk while the doctor walks them out. They put something on the books six months from now and smile politely at the receptionist. They hold it together all the way down the stairs and out into the parking lot.

I-Wanna-Live brings the car around and doesn't get their hopes up.

This time they both really lose it.

"I don't wanna do it anymore!"

Please-Put-Me-Out-Of-My-Misery wails and pulls at their hair. A matryoshka of breakdowns into bigger breakdowns. A real sight to behold.

"Don't make me. Not one more day. Not one more fucking day, please. Please, please if you really loved me you'd put me out of my misery. Please just let me die I can't do this anymore. I don't wanna do it."

I-Wanna-Live just slams their hand against the steering wheel over and over again, screaming, "You can't! You can't! You can't!"

That was where the insomnia started. That was the first time *I-Wanna-Live* stayed awake the whole night in a chair in the kitchen holding a shotgun, just listening. Waiting.

SURVIVAL EXHIBIT 246

I Get Stung By a Jellyfish

I parade into town to show off my jellyfish cape. Delicate tendrils hang around my neck, wrapping around my arms, tangled in my fingers. It shines iridescent blue in the sun. I spin and it gives the illusion of a necklace; some irresponsibly expensive piece known only by designer name and year. Red carpet stretches for miles around me in a radiating elegant shimmer. As I move, the jellyfish swims in rippling pulses through our frosted glass reflection.

When I show you, you scream.

I shrink away from your outstretched hands, stumbling backwards across the wet packed sand and into the rising waves. You're making such a fuss over this. It's fine. Really. It's fine.

"It's not *that* bad!" I think I sound believable. But when you move towards me again, I take a step back.

Now, there is not only pity, but hurt in your eyes.

"You have to let it go," you say.

And I know that. I look down at the stingers embedded in my skin. My body consumed by new blue veins. I know what you're saying is true, but it feels ever so slightly out of reach. Like my brain has put that knowledge up on the top shelf, too high for me to get.

And I want to let it go. I do not want to beg. Though I'm thinking I might have to, judging by the look on your face. The privilege of a swift death has already been taken from me. And the very thought that I have to survive this is too bright: it's like staring into the sun, I can't stand to look directly at it.

Years later—in the interview for the critically acclaimed television series *I Don't Know How I Survived*—they'll ask you how you knew what to do. You'll give most of the credit to instinct. You never mention how I cradled that soft transparent jellyfish body against my neck. You don't talk about what it was like to pull me apart.

"You can let it go now."

I squint into the sun and start begging.

The whole time you keep talking to me. I can't process a single word of it, but the cadence of your voice remains steady and unwavering. I think you are apologizing, as you pin my body to the sand. I am trying to apologize, too, even as I'm doing everything I can to break loose. I hit you, blindly and desperately, aiming for anywhere I can reach. This only drives the specialized stinging cells deeper into the soft tissue. I know this. The instinct to struggle is too strong. You do not let me go.

The tendrils peel off like they've been superheated and branded to my skin. When they finally do come away it's in wrenching, pulling fits and starts. What's left is red and ruined, leaking a thin clear oil.

For every barb pulled away there is another. More and more radiating pains that only really start to scare me once they feel distant. I start to feel distant. I'm watching the long blue arms hold onto me like they don't want to be separated. Unwoven.

It's taking long jagged peels of my skin. Ripping chunks out of me. The water does not run red with blood. Only pale swirls of pink from my bitten tongue, my split lip. This particular kind of venom destroys the cells from the inside, wreaking biological mayhem. I am torn up. I don't stop begging; for death or mercy and to remember if there had ever been a difference between the two before they were torn apart from each other.

It takes a long time.

Finally, the fight goes out of me. Somewhere along the way you had started praying. You were begging me to quit screaming. But when I do actually go silent, you realize the stillness is much worse. You miss the thrashing.

The pleading lays down into an incoherent mumble. I can't do anything but let you hold my head up out of the incoming tide. Each breath is arduous, gasping through the kelp-like stench of my own rotten lungs. The saltwater threatens to rush up over my face. You love me so much you do not listen when I ask to be held under.

Jellyfish stings like this are almost always fatal. Even with a proper medical staff, recovery requires a potentially lethal dose of painkillers. Then the removal of every single microscopic stinger involves the use of razor blades to scrape them from the skin. The few survivors unanimously agree that removal was significantly more traumatic than the initial sting. One ichthyologist described the ordeal as being "as bad as it can get without actually leading to death."

Eventually, I am silent. This is the moment it first occurs to you that I really might not make it. Even after all this. Even with a hospital's worth of hands to hold me down there is a chance I don't survive. That I might get soaked in vinegar and filled with drugs and then die anyway. The doctors will take razors to scrape the remaining stingers from my remaining skin and it will be for nothing.

I ask you with just my eyes if I'll live through this.

You're crying too much to say anything at all. The shredding never never seems to stop. No matter how little of me there is left.

Can you—do you blame me? For when I went so away I couldn't even help?

Do you think we'll make it?

SOSSRIY

SOSSRIY

SO
SORRY
SO
SSRI
SO SO
SOS
SSOSS
SOSOSO
RRY
RRI
SORRY
SOSSRI

SOSSRI
          SO
                    SOS
                              SOSRRY
                                        SOSRRI
                                        SO
                                        SO

                    SOSS

                              SOS

                                        SOS

                                                  SORRY

                                                            SOSOSSRIY

SO

SOS

SOSRRY

SOSRRI

SOSSRIY

SO

SO
O

SURVIVAL EXHIBIT 72
Golf Pencil

I-Wanna-Live calls the suicide hotline.
I-Wanna-Live sits in the church parking lot and prays,
humming along to the hold music.

I-Wanna-Live drives herself to the Sike Ward.
I-Wanna-Live exhales into the breathalyzer
pushed through the barred window by a crisis worker.

I-Wanna-Live is still while security wands her down.
I-Wanna-Live pees in a cup and
checks boxes on the intake form.

I-Wanna-Live watches a social worker take her belongings.
I-Wanna-Live sits in the waiting room,
stares dead-eyed at a trashcan across the hall.

I-Wanna-Live takes out her earrings.
I-Wanna-Live strips down while two nurses watch
then swallows the plastic cup of pills they hand her.

I-Wanna-Live does jigsaw puzzles and
writes in her journal with a golf pencil.
I-Wanna-Live doesn't make eye contact for six days.

Please-Put-Me-Out-Of-My-Misery is at vising hours every day
to stare across the table at *I-Wanna-Live.*
They do coloring sheets and sit in silence.

SURVIVAL EXHIBIT 6,274,929

In Search of The One

Dear Adderall,

I miss you every time I hold a receipt in a grocery store. Fuck the recession, fuck the inflation, fuck the op-eds and financial advice. You were the one and only thing that made life livable. I saved so much money on not buying food it was almost what-a-*way*-to-go. That's like dying on a bungee jump. Now that's hyperactive. That's the way my heart goes taut whenever you would pick me up and laughing swing me round.

Dear Celexa,

During the divorce with Trazadone, I started taking acting classes. I wanted to get better at acting and worse overall.

Dear Sertraline,

They still call the name Zoloft in the waiting room. Zoloft in a cattle crush. In the uncomfortable pleather chair opposite an opulent desk and wall of expensive framed diplomas. Dr. *Starched-Pressed-Collar* who has never touched an iron unless it was for branding. For re-branding. For mark-downs. If it's the last thing he does, he'll sell you on it.

Dear Nothing,
I was with you so long I started writing odes to Depression.

Dear Lunesta,

You were a tiny time machine the pharmacy sold for four dollars a pop. Sometimes something small takes six months away from me. Takes years off my life. I said nothing in the entire world felt safe and you swallowed my car keys. When I said I would do anything to survive, you never let me live it down. How many nights did I tell you that I wanted to die, and how many times did we both forget by morning?

Dear Vyvanse,

You were a whole amusement park, on the day of a death. News crews cropping up everywhere, everywhere you look: black tarps popping up in the parking lot.

Dear Venlafaxine,

We don't talk anymore, but I'd still trust you to clean my room out. We're *gets to see my browser history* kind of tight. For you I'd give up my best hiding spots, my most secret stashes, everything that's under the false bottom drawer of my heart. Please understand—this is the highest declaration of love I can offer.

Dear Citalopram,

You were my very first love. My favorite. If you'd ever take me back I would run with you in an instant. Say the word. Say the word and I'm gone.

SURVIVAL EXHIBIT 504

Love, Depression

I work Christmas straight through New Year's
and this is the thanks I get?
Not a single sick day.
Only solemn whispers of vacation.
All this time, not so much as a solitary smoke break.

It's not like I get any recognition
for being the last one to sleep
and the first one awake.
Every
Single
Day.
But sure, Joy gets weekends off.

Joy clocks out early.
Joy barely shows up for birthday parties.
Joy went and Rage quit weeks ago with no notice,
Hope hasn't shown their face in months,
Optimism joined a cult and went no contact.

You think the whitecoats are a match for me?
With their prescription pillbox of soldiers
and workbooks for mindfulness and guided meditation?
They are but bugs upon my windshield.

I am your oldest companion, your closest friend.
I have never once feared death.

SURVIVAL EXHIBIT 804

Visiting Ours

I buy her the expensive, heart-shaped soap
she destroys it into floral bits.
I kiss across her knuckles, and when
she shows me her teeth
there are chips of nail polish stuck in her gumline.

She asks for salt.
I get her salt.
Glass jars of pink Himalayan crystals,
smooth wooden keepers and grinders,
cardboard canisters with easy pour metal spouts.
A twenty-pound bag of winter de-icer.

While dinner cooks, I pretend it's a strip steak.
Melted butter, I tell her, grated garlic,
and whatever the fuck rosemary is.
We'll split something with the bone-in,
dusted with that fancy flake salt

You'll laugh with me and forget about the crushing.
You won't get any smaller.
I won't dissolve into the way you hold my face,
the way you care for a wound.

Lick the tears from my eyes.
Suck my bleeding fingers into your mouth.
The closest I'll get to curing, I think,
is if you eat me, sweetly, with salt.

Top 10 Chandeliers to Be Crushed By

10. The art museum has a big crystal one that's shaped like a skull & cross bones and I think that would be the best chandelier to be crushed by. It'd be so funny. Pictures of the blood smear would go viral.

9. There is a ceiling made of Jewel Beetles. In the Royal Palace of Brussels hangs a green chandelier that artist Jan Fabre covered in over one million tiny emerald wings. It took three months to place each individual beetle wing by hand.

8. Everything is a chandelier if you really think about it. The sun is a chandelier, and so is the moon. The North star is a chandelier. I am a chandelier and you are a chandelier. The pain you feel in your knee that reminds you of how quickly you are dying is a chandelier. Your dinner is a chandelier. The study of rot is a chandelier. Your new piercing is a chandelier. My baby teeth are a chandelier. At night when I pray for god to spare me, his mercy is a chandelier swinging over me.

7. Twice a year the very expensive Georgian crystal glass chandeliers at the Assembly Rooms are lowered towards the floor for cleaning and maintenance. They each hold 40 candles, and if they're all lit at once it totals over 400 open flames. In a past life it was my job to light them all. Hold my hands and tell me what they feel like.

6. The counter weight that holds the chandelier at the Paris Opera House weighs more than I do. The Chandelier itself weighs seven tons. It's killed before. It will do so again.

5. If you look up "chandelier" on IKEA.com there are 223 results in less than a second. None of them make the top ten.

4. In Vegas, among other things,there is something called a chandelier bar. You could be dead there three days before anyone ever even knew. You could stay slumped over in a swivel stool for a long time before anyone reported the smell. The spiral lattice of crystal prisms bounding down around your decaying corpse. The plinking of little glass beads. A snapped string heralding a very expensive rain.

3. It is entirely possible to reach the end of your rope and stay there. People who do not know the end of their rope think it must be some final step, but it isn't. You can stay there for years—build a home and a life full of simple little pleasures and very little rope. Do you know what the end looks like, for you? Do you remember being ten years old holding the mechanic's lamp for your father while he peered under the hood of a car?

2. From French *chandelle* and Latin *candela* meaning to glisten. Glisten: a visual onomatopoeia, glistening is just what a candle does. Why not hang hundreds.

1. I wear my grandfather's watch for sentimental reasons. If there is a way to wear a dead grandfather's dead watch for unsentimental reasons, I do not know it. The band is leather. The notches stretched to the exact size of his wrist. It no longer functions as a time-keeping device. It does not track my heartrate. Or my step count. Or my blood sugar or respiration or voicemail or unopened email or search history or porn preferences or upcoming appointments or estimated date of death. But I wear my grandfather's watch because it makes me feel like more of a man.

0. If you stand directly under the heaviest chandelier in Saint Peter's Cathedral, the security guards will start to get suspicious, eventually. You will make them nervous. Even though you're not doing anything wrong. You are making everyone uncomfortable, but that's not technically against the rules. It's not like you're loosening screws or anything— you're just standing there, hoping to be crushed.

SURVIVAL EXHIBIT 13

Good Housekeeping

I-Wanna-Live is on a cleaning kick. This means Whitney Houston's chart-topping hit "I Wanna Dance With Somebody (Who Loves Me)"is at full volume. This means immaculate countertops. The closet contents have been dry-cleaned and ironed and organized by season. *I-Wanna-Live* is emptying out another makeup bag, swatching lipsticks down one arm to check if they've dried out. The whole house smells eye-burningly of lemon.

Please-Put-Me-Out-Of-My-Misery didn't sleep well. *Please-Put-Me-Out-Of-My-Misery* can't get out of bed.

They both know a bad sign when they see one. It's just that too much time in bed is safer than the alternative.

"Come on," *I-Wanna-Live* tugs at the untucked corner of the bedsheets. "You'll have to get up, eventually, if I'm going to wash these. Come on."

"I don't want to."

"Well, if you're gonna get better you'll have to."

"I don't. Want."

"You don't want? To get better?"

"I don't want anything at all."

SURVIVAL EXHIBIT 404

On a Scale of 1-10

The pain scale is not designed for negative integers. Negative pain is a buffer overrun. That means the amount of data in the buffer exceeds storage capacity in such a way that causes the excess data to overflow into adjacent memory locations and corrupts or otherwise overwrites what is already there.

In the simplest terms:
negative pain
is when a vessel
bursts,
you get blood all over
your good memories.

SURVIVAL EXHIBIT 911
Career Suicide

My job is to not press the button.

It's not the most exciting thing to talk about at parties. There are only so many ways I can recount the riveting single thing I do for work: I do not press the button. That is the only rule. The job description was also the new hire orientation. All in one. Sometimes when I try to explain it, people are polite enough to laugh.

Maybe it would be better if it were at least a button I *could* press.

It's something about the negative objective that makes people uncomfortable. If my job were to press a button day in and day out—or hell, several buttons—they'd say okay you work at a factory or something. They'd understand that. But the absence of any end product makes them uncomfortable. Weary of me. Suspicious that my job isn't real. But it's not like preventative care isn't a perfectly respectable career path. The whole point of a security guard is for them to be there even when nothing is going wrong. It's not like the secret service is hounded because their responsibility is to make something *not* happen. Plenty of trades trade on inaction.

It's honest work. Work that I am good at, not through some natural born talent, but because I have practiced. I am *practiced*. I haven't broken yet. Sure, take any average Joe from his office and he'll tell you he could do it. But he wouldn't last a week. He'd have thrown in the towel years ago. Would have caught one glimpse of some slimy trail of blood, and without even discovering what left it behind, he would have slammed that button so hard it shook the building. I do a good job. I stay strong.

I know sound doesn't travel far from the basement. Once you get to the second or third floor you can barely hear the screams at all. The threatening letters slipped under my office door do not intimidate me. Even if they are all in my handwriting. I do not listen. I do not press the button. I know what leaves the bloodstains. It doesn't matter how much I beg. How much anyone begs. I do not press the button.

This job saves lives. Or at least one life over and over again every day that I do it. What does that count for? Seriously. Unrhetorically: what does that count for? HR won't tell me. HR won't even talk to me anymore. HR stopped returning my calls years ago. I can only guess at the amount of vacation time I have accrued. The 401k limit here is insane. Not that it matters, though. That's the thing with this job, there is no retirement. No time off. It's every waking moment. Constant vigilance on that button. For every day I slog through I am rewarded with another. I've been thinking about quitting, though I'll probably stay.

There is no clocking out of this. Well, there is. But it breaks the very first rule of the job.

SURVIVAL EXHIBIT 1111

If I Had Been Successful

I wouldn't have taken the whole
bus ride back just to talk to you
you never would have opened your mouth
licked the pad of your thumb
and used your saliva to stick
the temporary tattoo to my face
I wouldn't have biked home
covered in little fluffy bits of your feather boa

I wouldn't have taken
the walk when I didn't want to
and the woman I remember mostly as bruise
wouldn't have stopped me to ask for a tampon
If I had been successful
there would be no one to check in on your dad
no one crying in any of my top ten parking lots to cry in
one less member of the grateful-for-failure club
If I had been successful

I wouldn't have
your handwritten card
digesting in my stomach
I wouldn't have eaten it
to teach my body a lesson on
metabolizing sweetness
If I had been successful

I wouldn't
be here
if

I
go
belly up and hopeless
who will dig an elbow into the bare skin of your shoulder?
A ghost
can't work the knots from your back

Suicidal Ideation and Reality Television

On the show *Survivor*
they make you do something called "The Last Gasp."
The producers call it an endurance challenge
but it's basically drowning.

They boat you out to the middle of the ocean
and you swim under a metal grate
face pressed against the bars staring into the sky.
You fit easier now that you've been eating nothing but rice.
The last one to tap out wins their weight in food.

The waves come up to your
chest then
shoulders then
neck then
mouth then
nose then
over

The host narrates from his raised platform,
"You have to dig deep,"
he says.
"How bad do you want this?"
he asks.
"Is the pain setting in yet?"
It is.
"Can you go somewhere else in your mind?"
You follow him home to his luxury apartment in Los Angeles
and crawl into his big soft bed and vomit up half-digested rice.

When high tide comes in
it keeps you completely underwater for each wave.
You hold on. You hold on.
You have to hold on.
You have left your body.
You are a little glitter in the vast sea
having been reassured the tide will go back out again.

Breathing when you can
and praying when you can't.
Reduced to spitting up saltwater.

Upon My Passing

You tell me about your panic with the way you put the key in the lock. The exact same pattern of motion and sound. You are almost always silent. You tell me about your panic with the thrown phone. Only onto soft surfaces because you can't afford not to. Black glass rectangle smudged with the oils of your hands. The new necklace tells me about your panic. The jewelry gone sharp and unfeminine again. Spikes ringed around your throat so you know no one can grab. Hair kept so short you know no one can grab. You will not buy an extra lock. You say what's the point.

You are livid when I show you the wounds. I don't remember where I picked up that word. The way I don't remember where I learned I shouldn't put up certain fingers—raise the hem of my shirt or my voice. Livid, who sounds like a living relative, you squint. Livid with a face that anger taught you to shave. The wounds get antibiotic ointment and aloe. I get you to let livid go from between your teeth. And it seems more survivable, somehow, now with the good dog of Sorry asleep at our feet. Sorry curled between us on the bed, chasing rabbits in its dreams. Bright green Velcro vest I follow where it leads. Sorry, my soft service animal.

I find you on the garage floor in the dark. I keep saying *please* because it is the most familiar word. I pin you to the floor: half with my body but mostly with *please.* Dropped soda cans rolling in all directions. I don't know a word that means thirsty and dying like starving does. *Dehydration. Heat exhaustion. Parched* or *chapped,* but there is nothing. I have no name for the thing closing up over your head. There is only thirsty with extra emphasis. You close a hand around my wrist—not even to stop me trying to drag you towards the light. You smile at me. The tape of *please* flips over. Your face tipped over. That one rare moment of clarity already gone. Evaporated from the skin around your eyes. Flaking in the creases of your face. *What did you do?* And you laugh. You laugh, and no matter how many times I say *please* I'm not in on the joke. *What did you do?* You blink up at me. "I was in so much pain." *I was in so much pain.* You say it again. You say it again and again until we repeat it back to one another. End up passing it between us like a breathing tube in the dark. Like a joint. Like a bottle. The umbilical-cord carries nothing but blood. We are divers sharing deep breaths. Needing up, but not too fast.

You put on a good front for the doctors. You hold my hand in the waiting room. You come back and sit on the extra chair. Doctor sees me in the appointment sense. Doctor checks boxes. Doctor chants sleep cycle, appetite, comprehension, productivity. Device goes in each ear. A hand sweeps over the throat. Doctor charts cuticles, follicles, scalp and gumline. Doctor says the tri-cyclic antidepressants are to be treated like a loaded gun. Doctor says buy an extra lock. You google OSDD, NDA, NPO, TMS, ECT, EMDR, DNR. The Doctor frowns at me. "You ever been on Lexapro?" I nod. "Welbutrin? Trazadone? Venlafaxine? Prozac? Fluvoxamine?" I nod. I nod. I nod. I nod. I nod.

You wait in the field behind the parking lot and watch me walk in and out of work every day for two whole years. You rattle the fence and scream at the sight of me. You yell: "I'M TWENTY-EIGHT!" Even when it isn't true. For a time it is true. Twenty-eight is a parade down Main Street and I am leading the way. Twenty-eight is my favorite celestial body. Twenty-eight is a natural state of decay; a memory that belongs in the ground but also in the sky. Just once, you came close enough for me to touch. Offered unburned arms, unpeeled fingers, unblackened eyes. For me, this private reverse-stigma. You with a soft scalp free of scabs. I run my hands through your hair, twisting this way and that. Laughing, somehow, as you show me your long unbroken nails.

In the thin office, Sike says I have to name one good thing about myself. I am alone in the waiting room, wishing it were a restaurant that loved me with its loudness. I wish the waiting room were a fork I could clatter to the floor so I could say *thank you* when someone hands it back to me. I tell you about my hurt with the way I cannot get the words around it. *I'd do anything anything anything to make this pain go away.* You tell me about your panic, love, with the way you're doing rescue breaths from all the way over there. Silent for so long that years pass before I do. Years go by before you ask me "Even live through it?" Now Sike repeats the question. I must name one good thing about myself, and I am sure silence is the worst answer. Until I actually open my mouth. *I'm not giving up.* As if, at this point, persistence isn't the cruelest imaginable thing.

Post-Lobotomy Care Instructions

When I return home after the lobotomy my soap smells different.

Not any less floral, just like I have suddenly remembered what soap is made of.

And the television only gets one channel. Dr. Phil re-runs all day.

Something used to be here. A shadow. Like when I brought my car in for an oil change, and after re-entering the familiar space, all the seats were moved and the radio pre-sets were different. I listened to the same two radio stations for years. Now I can't remember the right string of numbers. They're gone.

I take the dog on walks. Fresh air is supposed to help. My skin turns pink in the sun.

I wash my sheets. I'm supposed to eat more protein and root vegetables. Take iron supplements.

There is something sharp, rattling around inside my head now. Mindfulness is supposed to help. Something that the inside of my skull cannot sand down. It only opens more wounds.

I think she gave it to me.

She saved me. When I was in the hospital she stood at the foot of my bed, some fluffy thing balled up in her hands, and she said, "Do you want a blanket that smells like home?" and it didn't even matter that the blanket smelled like her home and not my home, just that it wasn't a thin sheet that made me think of dead skin cells and lemon disinfectant. I owe her. She altered my brain chemistry. She changed me. When I think of my happy place, I know hers is right next door. She saved my life. I love her. I'll never see her again.

I can't remember what she looked like. Yoga is supposed to help. I don't even know her name.

SURVIVAL EXHIBIT 76,338

I Get Put Under Anesthesia and Not All of Me Comes Back

Please-Put-Me-Out-Of-My-Misery is having a good day. Up when the sun was. Got dressed in what real people call real people clothes and left for the doctor's office on time.

I-Wanna-Live rides shotgun. Suspicious.

No one says anything about last night. *I-Wanna-Live* just looks at *Please-Put-Me-Out-Of-My-Misery* smiling for once, holding a travel mug of hot tea and singing along to the radio.

They're going so fast.

Ode to My Big Dumb Gay Heart

There is a world in which I do not wear cool boots.
In that world, I never cut my hair short,

my feminine fits just fine.
My wedding was probably wonderful.

In that world, I am still sad,
but the normal kind

where it's just another emotion
that I feel occasionally and in manageable amounts.

In that world, I have never cried in a classroom,
I do not sit for hours in my parked car.

There, my Heart is not a former fighting dog.
There, my Heart is not a half-filled mylar balloon.

That is the world all the childhood games of MASH promised me,
where I'm good at things. Important things.

Impressive things. Things that make money.
There is a world in which I have a retirement plan.

In that world, I lead my soft Heart out into the woods.
I don't look back when it chases me, wailing.

When my Big Dumb Gay Heart keeps finding its way back,
I blow its brains out.

In that world, when I kill myself,
no one reads poetry at my funeral.

But in this world,
I am still here
to do it myself.

SURVIVAL EXHIBIT 27
Palliative Self-Care

At my old work we sold pocket-knives.

Switchblades. Butterflies. Balisong. A line of fancy green and purple box cutters. They've all got names. Inoffensive, corporate-chosen callsigns distinguishing the different styles. Usually they're foreign mountain ranges or large predatory animals.

Not like the leather gloves we stock in the winter. They are all called delicate feminine things like they're Victorian ladies. Gloves named Tiffany. Or Caroline. Or Ada or Elizabeth or Violet or Claire.

I name the spiders in the backroom. They're my constant companions who don't mind the same six songs on the store radio. I sweep up their webs. I name them after pop stars. Spider-Madonna spins a new home in the corner by the coffee maker. Spider-Rihanna moves in under the mop buckets. I am never brave enough to smash them. The knives stare at me all day from under the scratched display case glass.

I make an hourly wage of not-enough-to-pay-rent. I am paid to stand there with the master keyring twisting in my hands while men hold up bushcraft axes. Small handled hatchets. Carpentry tools sheathed in vegetable-tanned leather. Splitting mauls hauled up to the light for inspection. They pull their thumbs along the sharp lines. I bring out a bottle of bleach for the blood, and they tell me about shaving with a straight-edge. My one and only performance evaluation calls me polite and helpful. I am polite and helpful. It doesn't get me a raise.

I do not tell my boss about the man who bought two forest axes and took off his leather belt in a way that scared me. Or the man who backed his car out and didn't even see me. Or the man who came squealing through the opening shift-silence doing eighty in a thirty-five. Brakes shrieking. Break room filled with acrid smoke. I smell like burning rubber for the rest of my life. I am smart. I know to smile. I run his card and hand over his receipt. I wish him a good rest of his day while crumpled safety glass sprinkles down out of my hair. I thank him.

I do not tell my boss about the bird I carry out of the store using the rubber cleaning gloves and a paper bag. I never mention my brittle bones. Or the little boy who hit the glass door so hard the corner that we never clean was covered in his blood. I'm fourth generation self-taught on how to get stains out. I am smart. I know to smile. I never tell. My boss never asks me why I didn't say anything. I never admit to anyone that I am most ashamed of my relief. Of how fucking lucky I feel. Not everyone gets to be both hit and run. It's not until three months later when I'm in the middle of an inventory report that it even occurs to me that asking the man to leave had been an option. When my boss asks why I'm crying I tell him I'm afraid of the spiders. Next time I clock in Spider-Britney Spears is a stain.

I buy a knife named after the Viking god of wind and call her Selena instead. Selena sleeps at the foot of my bed. I am holding Selena's hand when my neighbor catcalls from across the parking lot. I wake up to Selena tangled in my sheets. She stays under my pillow until a man wearing a mask comes into the store. Then I start bringing her to work.

When a man with no shoes asks me for a Sharpie and a cardboard box, I get written up. When a homeless man steals a sleeping bag, I lock myself in the bathroom to cry. The bathroom is miles away. I have to go through the hotel lobby next door to get to it, ask security at the marble front desk for a little electronic key, and then beep myself in like it's a government building instead of a toilet. No one ever catches me crying there. Or anywhere.

I never have to do anything but small-talk security until one winter night when a man refuses to leave after closing. He wanders the store unzipping all the jackets. He screams when he sees Spider-Kelly Clarkson crawl out of a shoebox. My co-worker goes next door to get security and I watch the man make a stain of Spider-Kelly Clarkson. Security stands by the main doors and makes sure no merchandise is stolen. We huddle behind the cashwrap and thank him. My coworker calls the police but before they arrive and shoot the man, I have talked him back out into the night using my *schoolteacher* voice.

I make it back for two-and-a-half more shifts. Then—the very moment I realize it is an option—I quit.

I keep Selena in my bra. Tucked against skin and the thick bottom band of elastic. I buy exercise shorts with extra pockets. I get a window-puncher and run with it tucked in my knee-high socks. I fill my top two drawers with *Anti-Assault Underwear.* I sign up for self-defense-slash-speed-dating. Selena and I paint the town. Death swears to take me out soon but just stood me up again. I go on blind dates and to underground fighting rings. I go back to Debt's place and we make out on his couch. I polish Selena while sitting in my bathtub. I read that carrying a weapon you don't know how to use only puts you in more danger. I buy another knife. Then a taser.

I spend two weeks' worth of pay on a new skin care routine: dermatologist approved acne scrub, a glass jar of retinoid cream, skin toner, rose water, anti-aging lotions, tiger's eye gua sha sculpting tools, a jade face roller, translucent powder, and lavender-infused setting spray. I buy expensive face masks. I sleep in my childhood bedroom, which is also my bedroom now. I sit on the bleach-stained carpet while Selena cuts into the colorful packaging of a sea salt sheet mask. I watch Spider-Ke$ha crawl along the wall. Spider-Taylor Swift retreats back into the window well. I stay there until the chemicals soak into my skin. Until I am cold and trembling. Until the paper-visage is dry and spent. Then I peel it away from my face. I cut it into tiny pieces and one by one I pop them into my mouth and eat them.

Standing Offer to Eat Fingers

In dedication to the chiropractor who told my mother
that losing weight would cure her chronic pain.
She tells me about him over dinner,
and after I finish my second slice of pizza
I drive to his house and I bite off all his fingers.

I get all the digits of the biggest names in Hollywood.
I lie in wait at their mansions.
I serve them little cocktail weenies on their yachts
set to a soundtrack of non-stop punk-rock girly-pop.
I cast these men in my amateur Saw film.

When a classmate body blocks me
with *doesn't he get a hug?*
I do not give it to him.
I bite all of his fingers off instead.
When a customer at my fast-food job
does not ask for my consent,
I do not hide in the walk-in freezer to weep.
I launch myself over the counter to bite off his fingers.
When my blind date makes some comment about the waitress,
I engage in a civilized and nuanced conversation about
boundaries—
Just kidding, I bite his fingers off!

I run a public service:
when someone you know has lost their finger privileges,
you know who to call.
I'm your friendly neighborhood specialist in unhinging.
Go on, put some fingers in my mouth.

In this poem, as in real life,
my teeth are so, so sharp.

SURVIVAL EXHIBIT 296.3

Safety Planning

"And do you? Have a plan?"

I have hope for the first time in years and it's shaped like a chasing hammer.

But that isn't what Dr. *Fancy-Name-Plate* means when asking if I have a plan.

He means, do I have a friend militant enough to reliably pick up the phone at all hours? Do I have someone who will hate me back to life? Do I have a sweet old person in my life and can I imagine what they'd wear to my funeral?

Dr. *Fancy-Name-Plate* means, have I seen the most recent season of the smash-hit reality show, the one where blue collar workers compete for a cash prize? The one where—in competition for a new pickup truck—a man uses a post-driver to pound metal stakes into the packed dirt. Except he's throwing his weight into the wrong technique, so instead of sinking deeper into the dirt the steel is beginning to bend. No matter how hard he brings the driver down, the stake only continues to warp and he's getting nowhere. He's crying. The audience saw a picture of his two little girls in the opening montage, and he's still bringing the post-driver down again and again. His teammate—who, by the rules of the challenge, is unable to help—stands at the other end of the field framed by the most yellow sunset imaginable, and all she can do is scream. *Hey! Hey look at me. Don't you throw in the towel yet. You're not gonna give up. You can't quit, you hear me?*

And when Dr. *Fancy-Name-Plate* asks if I have a plan, he means, do I have a post-driver. Means, do I have anything sharp in the drawer of my bedside table? Means, do I have violence in the house and is it somewhere easy to reach?

"I'm allowed to hope, aren't I? I can have hope."

Dr. *Fancy-Name-Plate* sighs.

Dr. *Fancy-Name-Plate* watch-checks me.

"Ok. Here's what we're going to do—" but he loses me by the third word.

No doctor has ever said *we* and meant it in a way I understand.

SURVIVAL EXHIBIT 855,366

Ode to the Year With No Hope

January:

Make a new morning routine. First thing in the morning say *thank you*. Get up in the morning and say *thank you*. Be grateful. Show gratitude. In the morning, make a new morning routine. Get up early. Get up earlier. Get up. Get up. Get up!

February:

Labs come back normal.

March:

I never talk about it, but during the pandemic I become obsessed with roller coaster crashes. I too, had no incidents for over 20 years. I too, broke catastrophically. I hear the sirens from my window. I write the word *disaster* as many times as I can by hand in an hour.

April:

The airport chapel smells like piss. It's the only place god will talk to me. god says if I see a perfect sunset I've earned the right to leave the table. I've waited with the night sky for years.

May:

It gets better. (I believe it.)

June:

It gets better. (I want to believe it.)

July:

It gets better. (I've never wanted to believe anything so bad in my entire life.)

August:

Crash land on Depression's couch. Time loop living in the guest room. Sleep on Ideation's floor. The driver's seat is never where I left it. I leave and go nowhere. My therapist makes me pick up thirteen thousand pieces of glitter just to make a point. Survival is not a party popper. Survival is not a single broken seal. Survival is hands and knees picking glitter out of the carpet.

September:

A woman flags me down in the parking lot. She asks me to help load her groceries into the trunk, and if I hadn't taken an extra hour to cry in my bed before driving to the store we would have missed each other. I look at the way her trunk stands open, waiting for me. I swear off asking the universe for signs and load the bags into her car.

October:

I peel an inch-long strip of dry skin off my bottom lip. The dead shred of flesh wafts through the air and settles on the tiled floor. For weeks it lays there and cries.

November:

While deleting files off my hard drive, I find the video again. A 33-second clip of a spring blizzard from last year. I've stuck my phone out the cafeteria window to film the fat wet wads of snow coming down in the fading light. You can hear the kiddos giggling in the background. *"Look! Look!"* the youngest chants, and his brother looks. They press their faces to the glass and laugh.

December:

Dear god of indestructibility, thank you for making me indestructible. I am indestructible. I like a leather strip between my teeth. My first word every year is *HAPPY.* Happy happy happy. Happy New Year of happy didn't take. Happy New Year of nothing takes. Happy Year of sneering. Year of spitting blood. So? I wipe my face. So what's one more?

SURVIVAL EXHIBIT 1,409

Who is Curley's Wife if Not His Wife

While out setting rabbit traps I learn two things:

1. Grown men don't scream like big cats
   These men, howling, court pain
   But can't even recognize it without mascara

2. Pain has never been the most hurtful thing
   Hope
   Hope is the most painful thing

SURVIVAL EXHIBIT 470

Poem About Nature That is Also About Being Trans

Autumn has come back to me
in this one long hair
I found half knitted
into my scarf
that I know cannot be mine.

Ivy is growing new leaves again,
which means I hold her gently,
drive everywhere in silence.
Even the happy songs sound like
a call for help with sharp edges.

Juno loves everyone in the restaurant.
Juno's number never met a receipt it didn't want to flirt with.
Juno's heart is an emotional support Labrador
that fosters cheetah cubs.
Juno says *I love you*
more than Juno breathes.
Juno says *I love you*
more than Juno breathes.

April keeps me alive every year,
speaks my name into the mirror and summons me
to watch her do her makeup.
There are days we both manage smiles.

SURVIVAL EXHIBIT 71923

Ode to the Braincell

I don't know much,
but I know I love you.

Even when the brain cell
spends more time with you
I'm not mad.

I imagine him,
little workhorse stretched out in the shade
warmed by the sun in your head.
Seasalt tang under the edges of his nails.
He will come back smelling of your soap.

I think of you fondly
when our thoughts take
the wrong
train home.
Strangers
post concert
singing
on a platform

they don't even know isn't theirs
lost
and having the time of their lives.

Every New Engagement Announcement

i pick a Beatle's song i haven't heard and listen to it lying on my bedroom floor *DING!* with every new engagement announcement, i change the sound of my morning alarm *DING!* more than once the news of a new marriage pings across my screen while i'm cleaning my *DING!* own vomit off the floor while i'm at a hookup's house, i've got the windows down in my car *DING!* while i'm in the bathroom, and we're all praying i come back *DING!* alive while i'm living in a basement hoping i don't get *DING!* murdered for who i am. *DING!* when i'm at the beach ripping out of my own body with the grief that i ever wanted to leave *DING!* and without even pausing *DING!* for breath joy that i crawled through those miles of pain it took to be here right *DING!* now hooks dug as deep as they will go into this chance to live *DING!*

there's a wedding announcement
and i'm in my doctor's office begging
i'm lying in the grass being fed fruit
i'm writing a poem
about being so sad it's a near
death experience

DING! when i'm buying a bottle of wine at the grocery store and nothing feels real except for all the awful stuff that feels so fucking *DING!* real it's going to crush me but it's taking so *DING!* long i'm getting bored *DING!* of being crushed to death *DING!* someone i knew *DING!* in high school is getting *DING!* married and i spent *DING!* the afternoon *DING!* in the sun, *DING!* mourning the fact *DING!* that i will never be a teenage boy who is good at baseball.

Getting My Tubes Tied as Performance Art

I know the drill—
I know when Doc says pressure it means pain.
I know Sike will be by later to scrape me
for numbers.
PCP says it's just one little pinch
that I might regret given my age
or marital status
or the bill.

But I bring R—whom I love—to hold my hand,
and M—whom I love—to make me laugh while they tie me up,
and J—whom I love—talks about Boy Scout knots
and fly fishing,
and in the stirrups I want to be a soft pink bow.
Something exciting to undo with your teeth,
boom/crack reveal the color inside,
but L—whom I love—kisses my belly,
says

sunhat ribbon.

SURVIVAL EXHIBIT 303
Wish Fulfillment Center

The Lord God Almighty
Holy Spirit Incarnate
Jesus Christ Himself

descends from the Heavens to give me
a gold medal, a chocolate cookie,
and a scratcher card.

"Congratulations," he says.
I'd never seen a depiction of Christ
that got his gap-tooth just right.

He says "You have officially used up
all your suffering quotient. You have been in pain
for so long, my child, but now it is over."

Jesus Christ, he looks sheepish.
I think he was going in for a hug
when I put my hands out
to check him for knives.

SURVIVAL EXHIBIT 14

I Say I Love You on the First Date

I loved you when we were both girls
who didn't dance at the formal.
I loved you when you were the sad ending
of a movie I couldn't bring myself to hate.
When you were a teenage boy at a bake sale, and you were excited
by the damp wad of cash that had come from my bra,
I loved you.

I loved you when I was a river rock and your hand was the first warm thing
that had ever touched me.
I loved you when you were a baby and I was a lemon wedge.
I loved you when you were a TV special taped on VHS.
I was the type of blood that can be donated to anyone, and I loved you.
You were the dustjacket of a book on chronic pain, and I loved you.
We made lemon-poppyseed muffins,
and before they had even cooled, I loved you.

I love you
here and alive
like it is the greatest victory.

I say I love you on the first date.
It's the only thing I'm sure of.

Lobotomy Horse Protection Squad

Lobotomy Horse gets sent to a farm upstate.

Lobotomy Horse holds down a volunteer position at the local library. Lobotomy Horse eats Thanksgiving dinner from a paper plate out on the back porch.

The horoscope app that Lobotomy Horse downloaded predicts that the worst of the misery has already passed. This month is supposed to be lucky for love. Lobotomy Horse, in a fit of rage, smashes its brand-new smart phone under a concrete paver.

Lobotomy Horse is not a model recoveree. Lobotomy Horse cannot be unbroken. It stockpiles sharp things and ice cream. Lobotomy Horse is large and angry and violent. It still cries more days than not. If it had a more optimistic outlook on the treatment plan then maybe it would work.

Lobotomy Horse heard a starting gun go off and was jealous of the hollow shell that got to leave the empty chamber. Lobotomy Horse broke its leg on the racetrack and thought *finally, finally this is it.*

But it wasn't.

Lobotomy Horse tries denial as a gateway drug. Lobotomy Horse can get a thirty-day free trial of its new prescription as long as it hands over all its sensitive information to data miners. In the data graveyard there is a willow tree with swaying terabyte limbs. They put Lobotomy Horse into a hex editor. They found strings of unused data corresponding to emotions left dormant. Dr. *Four-Months-For-An-Appointment* suggests Lobotomy Horse should shed water weight and detox all its junk files. In the data graveyard there is a walnut tree with swaying terabyte limbs.

Lobotomy Horse is not allowed to hurt itself.

This rule keeps Lobotomy Horse safe—until Lobotomy Horse catches fire and suffers full-thickness burns rather than raise a hand against itself. No one wants to touch Lobotomy Horse. Lobotomy Horse is burning to death and it is not allowed to throw its own body against the ground.

Lobotomy Horse lights up the night. Lobotomy Horse turns to the camera, just a silhouette in the inferno. The audience is given a glimpse of that winning smile. The farm upstate goes down in flames.

Dear Senator, Come Kill Me Yourself

You want me dead so bad, it's *embarrassing.*
I cannot *believe* you are *so obsessed*
with what shoes I wear to the mall,
or where I pee at the gym.
Senator, I am going to be the gayest person in the grocery store.
There's not a damn thing you can do about it.

Tell me, how does it feel to be outsmarted by actual children?
'Cause when kids see me, they go "Why is your hair like that?"
and I say "Because I like it this way!"
and they go "Are you a boy or a girl?"
and I say "Whatever I feel like!"
and they say "Oh ok. Do you want to play dinosaur heroes with us?"
We could have a world where we all play dinosaur heroes together!
But *Nooooo.*

No, you're the reason I have to see my insurance company
post a fucking rainbow on Linkedin
along with a post about how the corporation is
"disheartened by the record-breaking year
of at least 525 anti-LGBTQ+ bills proposed across 41 states in 2023."

Dear Senator, I'm going to outlive you.
The amount of spite I have stockpiled will get me through every winter.
My Joy is an immortal, unkillable, endless, all-enduring, ever-abiding force to be reckoned with.

Not that you would know anything about it, but my Joy could eat you for breakfast.

Dear Donald Trump, Dear Ben Shapiro, Dear Tucker Carlson,
Alex Jones, Kristi Noem, Elon Musk, Mike Pence,
JD Vance, Jesse Watters, Megyn Kelly, Ted Cruz,
Rick Perry, Rick Santorum, Stephen Miller, Sean Hannity,
Sean Spicer, Bob Murray, Pam Bondi, Laura Ingraham,
and Mitch McConnell—bring your friends!

I can and will take on any of you
in hand-to-hand combat any day of the week.

Dear Senator, if you're really so hell-bent on eradication,
you will meet me in a Denny's parking lot,
you will fight me in a cage match,
you will look me in the eyes while you explain
why you don't care about my heartbeat anymore.
If you want me dead so bad you'd better come down here and do it yourself.

SURVIVAL EXHIBIT 33

Automatic Refill

god writes me a prescription
for $2 watery lemonade
bought at a stand from the neighborhood kids

god writes me a prescription
for poetry liquefied and fed
through a tube in my nose

god writes me a prescription
for rice cakes and root beer
and cashback at a respectable rate

god writes me a prescription
for getting laid or getting paid or
getting a lobotomy

god writes me a prescription
for new drugs that make it easier
to wean me off the other drugs

god writes me a prescription
for soap that smells like
I'm not missing anything

god writes me a prescription
for vitamin B
and bleaching the floors

god writes me a prescription
for I did all my dying up front
now it's all gonna be easy and gentle

god writes me a prescription
for I am fucked up in ways that haven't even been invented yet
and when they do find a cure, they'll give it my dead name

god writes me a prescription
for feeling like the biggest baddest
strongest motherfucker just for being alive

9 Times I Died and 1 Time I Didn't:

The first time I died was at a McDonald's during the lunch rush. The line of cars in the drive-through went all the way around the building, so I parked and went inside to order a Big Mac and fries. The teenager behind the counter called 911, but I was already gone. Right there on the grimy tile floor. I died thinking about how often they mopped. I died hungry.

Another time I got hit by a semi-truck. I was walking back to my dorm on a Friday and it ran up onto the sidewalk and crushed me under the front bumper. I didn't get a good look at the guy driving. Just the lower half of his face from under the sun visor. They said it was a heart attack that made him lose control of the vehicle. The rumor was that if your roommate died while school was in session then you got straight A's the whole year.

I died at a drag brunch. What a lovely way to go. Show so good I'm literally dead.

I died in the bathroom of a punk show. During the opener, I saw someone in the crowd who looked just like I used to. I watched her crowd surf. She was kind enough to let me stay for the whole show. Then, during the encore, she followed me into a stall and beat me with her bare hands.

One time my mother hugged me too tight and I crumbled into dust.

I fell down the steps at the MC Escher Museum and had a lot of time to think about my life before I hit the bottom.

I starved to death while hiding under your front porch. You didn't know I was there. We'd just had a fight because you saw a scar on my body. And you, all righteous and helpless, looked angry at the sight of it. Because we can barely look at each other, I couldn't tell if you were angry at me or what had been done to me. All I know is that you were mad. So I crawled under the front porch and haven't been able to get up.

Someone robbed the Dollar Tree and shot me. It was my fault, really. I didn't get down on the ground when he said to. I didn't do anything he said to. Just stood staring slack-jawed at the barrel of the gun. I'd gone in to buy some face masks and a new bottle of mouthwash. He said *do you wanna die,* and I just kept laughing so he shot me.

While soul-searching, I metaphorically fell into a thermal geyser. I was submerged up to the neck in symbolic boiling water and suffered third degree emotional burns on 90% of my body. I begged the whole night to die and in the morning, I finally did.

Plus one: I decide to live again while riding shotgun in her car. I do this all the time, the repeated dedication to being alive. The crushing realization that this is not the end. There are long stretches in my life in which the only thing I can do is keep myself alive. And sometimes not even that. Sometimes the only thing I'm good at is coming back from the dead.

3 New Inevitable Things: Queer Death, Gay Taxes, and Trans Joy

Queer Death

My gender: taking a dirt nap.
My name: sent to a farm upstate.
My pronouns: a bloody boxer and his beautiful wife.

I could never be a final girl but just maybe
I'll be the last sad bastard stumbling towards the light.

My grandmother says the prayer before dinner
and thanks god that we buried no children this year.
How lucky we are.
She doesn't know that she almost buried me this year,
and last year.
Every year
I am lucky
that there are 365 anniversaries
of the day I didn't die.

Gay Taxes

I tell my therapist
I saw the future
But not myself in it—
She checks her notes,
combs through the DSM5
to find a diagnostic code for
patient eats salads but still hates themself.

I call my accountant
and ask if there's a tax break
for wanting to die.

She suggests I fill out a W-2,
says loss of will-to-live
does not guarantee
an extension.

I ask a psychic
on the side of the road
if I will kill myself.

She consults her crystal ball,
pulls a card
and when she flips it over
the fool looks back at me.

I find a sticky note
stuck to my mirror
that says "Y'know,
just because you become unrecognizable,
doesn't mean that you don't make it."

Trans Joy

Just look at me.

List of things that saved my life

1. Costco rotisserie chicken

   A week and a half into treatment means the small victory today is chicken and broccoli for dinner. Pre-cooked from a plastic package, and it tastes like treatment is working. First bite like salt in the sixth century when it cost as much as gold. I had been kibble-fed before this, but Savor just slipped me a steak under the table. I didn't recognize Savor for the longest time. Even though he visits me every weekend. Sits by my bedside. Prays for my clear days. Savor spent years chanting *remember me remember me* and today I eat chicken and I do.

2. A single spool of navy-blue thread

   When I break the strap of my favorite purse from carrying too many books, my mother fixes it for me. She sews it by hand. Matches the thread color and everything.

3. Hard candy

   Mango flavored. Sike doc pulls a handful from a drawer and makes me take them. Thinks my name is *hospitalization*. Says she was praying that nothing happened to me. Can offer me a little packet of fake mango flavoring and sugar. The reminder of fruit while

I go away for six to eight weeks and we both hope I don't happen to myself.

4. Saying gay

In the parking lot of my old high school, I scream my lungs out. A metaphor being the only surgical removal I'm legally allowed. It's been months of bills up to my eyes and the only way to keep from drowning is saying *gay*. Until it means happy again. Until it means lifeboat. Until my pronouns are gay. My name is gay. Until I'm so gay I'm not allowed in the building. Gay. Gay Gay Gay Gay Gay. In a classroom here, I learned about aspen groves. Vast forests of lone trees interconnected by a single root system. They are one genetic individual. Can you feel it through our roots when I sit in my parked car and say *gay* because someone has to? Fellas, is it gay to be an aspen tree?

5. A sign from the universe

I ask the universe for a sign I should stay alive. My friend, when I tell her how sad I am on our weekly call, describes in vivid detail the dog walkers across the street. "It's just rained," she says, "they're all wearing matching green bandanas. All the dogs are leaving little paw prints on the sidewalk."

6. A SIGN FROM THE UNIVERSE

I ask the universe for a sign I should stay alive. That year for Christmas, my brother and I give each other the exact same gift.

7. Baby ducks

   I stop asking the universe for signs. Sometimes it's just too on the nose. When my girlfriend takes me to the park for a picnic on my birthday, there's a flock of tiny baby ducks dipping in and out of the sun-pinked water. It was just so obvious. The universe doesn't always talk to me, but when it does, it screams.

8. A bottle of wine that was a present from my neighbor

   I still don't know how to write a thank you card that says *I'm sorry, I was scared you were going to kill me.*

9. $6 scrub brush

   My clean closet. The empty dishwasher. The folded laundry. They are love letters. Signs of life. I am able to start living again. I start living again.

10. Not yoga

    Absent from this list: yoga, cutting out soda, nickel-free face wash, intermittent fasting, falling in love, getting a promotion, magnesium supplements, fish oil, raw cherry pits, changing my mindset, altering my attitude, synergizing, pushing myself, detox teas, ice baths, meditation playlists, creatine powder, jogging, and choosing happiness.

11. Prescription Ketamine

Ketamine plugged my brain back in. Turns out getting the medicine I needed was the cure for my sick brain. The light is bursting out of a darkened theater into the middle of a day I had no idea was even there. It is so easy to save my life. I do it all the time.

12. Refracted light

I don't know how I made it through the second round of washout week. The one I swore would be the last, but wasn't. I was on the clock and dying. Leaking through the breakroom drain grate. Night-sickness. Minimum wage brain zaps. Double masking. I vomited up my expensive lunch and didn't even get to go home early. And when I clocked out, the biggest brightest rainbow I had ever seen in my life. Ten minutes either way and I would have missed it.

SURVIVAL EXHIBIT 5119

Seat-Belt Law

Please-Put-Me-Out-Of-My-Misery and *I-Wanna-Live* go on a road trip.

Please-Put-Me-Out-Of-My-Misery and *I-Wanna-Live* get in a car crash.

An hour ago, at a rest stop, they were squabbling over which overpriced bag of snacks to buy, and now the little sour candies are scattered all over the road.

I-Wanna-Live lies face down in the dirt, watching the shattered bits of safety-glass reflecting light from a distant streetlamp.

It'd been maybe fifteen minutes since *Please-Put-Me-Out-Of-My-Misery* had gone for help.

They'd argued over it.

Please-Put-Me-Out-Of-My-Misery and *I-Wanna-Live* sprawled in a ditch screaming at each other, wasting time yelling about who had the better chance of climbing back up to the road. The bickering seemed like a sign nothing was too badly broken. In the middle of it, *I-Wanna-Live* started coughing up blood. There's nothing to say, after that.

They might not make it.

Even if *Please-Put-Me-Out-Of-My-Misery* does make it back to the car, it is no guarantee they will both survive. *I-Wanna-Live* keeps an emergency kit in the trunk, but a lukewarm bottle of water and a couple granola bars will only go so far. A cheap flare gun does not a rescue make.

I-Wanna-Live stays crumpled in a slowly melting bank of snow, counting the minutes manually. The pain, in the moment, is relatively small. The realization that it must be endured indefinitely is devastating.

I-Wanna-Live claws at the frozen gravel. Just to have something to focus on, just for the sensation of packed soil building up beneath their cracked finger nails. Just to distract from the future spooling out before them, a wilting daisy chain that promises no change and no relief. The worst part about dying is the crushing monotony.

I-Wanna-Live prays for relief and nothing changes.

I-Wanna-Live prays for relief and nothing happens.

I-Wanna-Live prays for relief and receives only more pain.

I-Wanna-Live prays for relief and gets none.

By the time *Please-Put-Me-Out-Of-My-Misery* comes stumbling back—covered in blood and mud and more wounds than before—there is no panic. Only a sucking sense of calm.

The prayer becomes desperate. That is when the begging starts.

Please-Put-Me-Out-Of-My-Misery doesn't have the emergency blanket, or the first-aid kit, or the half-empty bottle of Advil. They can't make it back up the road to the car. Can't get a signal on either partially-demolished cellphone. They're crying and shaking and saying sorry with every exhale. *Please-*

Put-Me-Out-Of-My-Misery presses their forehead against *I-Wanna-Live*'s and apologizes. *I'm sorry I'm sorry I'm so sorry it was an accident I swear I promise please please you have to believe me I didn't mean it just an accident I'm sorry.*

I-Wanna-Live lies in the cold mud and begs for death. *Please-Put-Me-Out-Of-My-Misery* holds them and prays for mercy. This goes on until there is nothing left to say but *please. Please please please.* They both just want this to end.

This goes on for so long that, it too, becomes boring.

Eventually they sink into silence. Low and dull and broken only by the birds perched along the telephone wires.

I-Wanna-Live grabs *Please-Put-Me-Out-Of-My-Misery* and hauls them in close. "Is this how it is, for you?"

Please-Put-Me-Out-Of-My-Misery looks at them. The gentle hand in their hair pauses.

There's a long silence, then: "What do you mean?"

Maybe they're starting to get it.

Maybe they're both starting to get it.

"Is this how *you always* feel?"

Prayer to the Patron Saint of Pain and Sadness

at the Pride parade I ate a lemon seed
so sour and cold
that it made me want to live again

SURVIVAL EXHIBIT 1,969

Positive Future Orientation

a hot chick reads my palm in the line for the bathroom
& says I will die during a commercial break
& that's why advertisements for online therapy
give me panic attacks

a lesbian gives me a tarot reading while weeping
& will not tell me why
nobody likes my party tricks
& my pause for laughter
following the most fucked up thing you've ever heard in your
life

a stranger on the train platform takes my pills
& swallows the same SSRIs that I do
& it feels more intimate than being married
hearing our drugs vocalize in search of each other

a queen at pride divines my future
she says we all go to Gay Heaven
yes even you
& the prophecy foretold someone
wearing a pride flag
will save my life
just by smiling at me

I never was a believer
until I find myself
in a mirror
& realize it is true

If This is a Medical Emergency, Please Hang Up and Dial 911

You cannot call witness protection
when you're the one who's trying to kill you.
By the time anyone ever even says the word suicide aloud,
the very concept of protection has been cold and in pieces—
dead under the back deck for months.

You cannot call in sick
to an oxymoronic urgent care
that only knows the word please
please please please please
see you in six months,
please come back and say it some more.

You cannot call your doctor
in the morning if there is none.
No more mornings at all,
only a prescription from the oxymoronic clinic
that your insurance doesn't cover.
You know you are loved you are so, so loved,
and the pain is unbearable.
This is not a contradiction.

You cannot call god
and give him a piece of your mind.
You cannot call the universe
cruel for letting you live
through times you wished you didn't.

You cannot phone a friend.
You cannot call animal control.
You cannot call poison control.
You cannot call an exorcist.

But you can call me,
and I will hold your hand.

I will hold you down
until hope catches up to us.

You will still think of hope as a rescue hound
come to give you warm kisses and a bottle of brandy.
You will still be under that impression until the very moment
hope gets its claws into you.

Hope is the world's greatest persistence hunter.
Hope will use its horns to gore you.
I will pin you to the floor. I will not let go
while hope gouges you open with its grotesque tusks,
and you
screaming and digging your nails into the soft skin of my face,
you will be disemboweled by hope,
eviscerated by hope,
devoured by hope,
made a hollow shell of yourself.

You cannot call hope
a stranger
when it crawls home into the steaming cavity of your body.
You will keep it warm enough to survive the night.

You can call me.

I will hold your hand,
and I will let you touch the scar
on my body. I will show you
what a wound like this becomes
once it heals.

Revenge of the Joy Wizard

I kidnap the Wizard of Joy and tie him to a kitchen chair. When he starts to come around I am sitting on the island countertop holding a knife.

"Y'know," I smile at him, "I met god, once."

We stare at one another for a long moment, each waiting for the other to speak while the silence of all silences descends upon the kitchen.

The Wizard of Joy never smiles at me. Now he fixes me with a look that says he is considering what my insides might look like splattered all over his nice wood stain cabinets.

I watch his eyes go from my face to somewhere back over my shoulder, leaning to the side in his chair to get a better look down the hallway at all the upended filing cabinets. I turned the Joy Wizard's house upside down in search of answers. His study, in the aftermath, resembles an impact crater. He cannot tell me anything I don't already know.

He has nothing for me.

I watch that realization—that he's in some truly deep shit—dawn across his face.

"God found out what I'd been doing." I hop down off the countertop and approach him. Slowly, knife held casually. "That I had been planning on destroying something that belonged to her."

"And god was..." The Joy Wizard flounders, as I come to a stop before him. He's not outright crying yet, but there are tears sticking his eyelashes together and when he blinks one slides down along the side of his nose. I watch him search my face for something, anything, that could help him. He does not find it.

"Merciful!" He scrambles for the words. "Right? God was merciful?"

"God handcuffed me to a folding chair." I reach down and skim a finger along the bottom of his chin then raise it until he's looking up at me. The move is reminiscent of how a lover might touch him. It is soft.

"God was not as kind to me as I will be to you."

He's weeping now. Quietly. Doing nothing to hide it.

"I know what it's like to beg for mercy." I kneel before the Wizard of Joy, my cheek rubbing against the expensive fabric of his pants. I settle with my chin resting on his knee. "When god threatened me, I cried. Just as you are now. Like an infant, who doesn't understand that no one is coming to comfort them."

The Joy Wizard trembles under my touch.

"Do you know what I could do to you?"

He doesn't, really. He has no idea what I'll put him through, though I'm sure his imagination is currently conjuring some ideas.

"I can give you names! Accomplices!" There is a delicious, desperate edge to his voice. Maybe there's still fight in him yet. It is possible that I underestimated the Wizard of Joy and his self-preservation instincts.

"Mercy!" He cries, all posturing forgotten now that he's begging. "And Peace! I can give you Peace! I know where Happiness lives!"

I pretend to consider it. Then stand over him and put my hands on the armrests of the chair.

"I don't want anything at all."

"Please! Please, what did you give god to let you go? What did you offer to escape unharmed?"

"Unharmed?" I lean over him, crowding into his space until we are eye-to-eye.

"God taught me," and god didn't let me go until I had learned, "that the will to survive can be torture. It is also love."

Even with our faces pressed this close together, I can't tell if the words strike him as familiar. They have become a sort of mantra for me.

"And have you figured it out yet?" He tilts his head, "what the difference is?"

That gives me pause. I hadn't.

Actually, it'd never even occurred to me that there was a measurable difference at all.

He catches some of that uncertainty on my face, delighted by my ignorance.

"You don't know!" He barks out a laugh. "That's what all this is about? You really are a few cards short of a full deck, aren't you?"

"Shut up," I remember the knife I have and press it firmly against his neck, "I'll cut out your tongue if I need to."

The Joy Wizard is undeterred.

"I'll do it. I will."

And he's still laughing. "*Christ.*" The Joy Wizard strains against his bonds with the force of his uproarious, raucous laughter. "Fucking hell, would it kill you to *lighten up?*"

Sike Ward

I met god
and she is me from the future.

She picks me up from prom
in a powder-blue suit and heels.

She takes me out back behind the woodshed
where we weep into each other's arms.

She comes up over the hill holding bolt cutters
while I am chewing off my own leg.

We
is the only word
she ever says.

Massive Poet Disaster

Three months on, and business at the café never really recovered. We lost a sizable chunk of management—though not anyone we had been *hoping* would suddenly drop dead—and our customer base took a big hit. Most of the regulars are gone. No more skittish teenagers with box-dyed hair. The man who rides the bright blue motorcycle hasn't been in, and I wonder what happened to his yappy dog. The gossips. The students. The knitting circle. All gone. Some, I assume, just started going to different coffee shops to avoid the embarrassment of being left behind in The Poet Rapture.

It's why, when the bell above the door announces a customer, I am expecting some insipid financier with a briefcase. But you, when you enter the coffee shop, look so artsy I am surprised you survived. I greet you with all the warmth and enthusiasm I can muster during a double shift. You smile anyway. Before, I would have wondered if you were a poet. Now I know you aren't, just given the fact that you are alive.

After some deliberation you order one of the fall specials and stand by the counter while I make it. When I hand you the to-go cup you are scanning the bookshelves along the far wall. We had a poetry section, but in the aftermath it got pulled. Supposedly management plans to create some sort of monument/display. No doubt it'll be my job to restack the books and arrange all the little *In Memoriam* cards. Make sure the grayscale author-photos are the first thing people see when they walk in the door. That, and a 25% off banner.

"Did you…" the question sticks somewhere inaudible, so you gesture to the barren bottom shelf in the corner. The books are more conspicuous in their absence than they ever were in their proper place. There's a shitty shrine of cardboard boxes taking up all the space in the supply closet. "Did you know anyone?"

The question isn't really about knowing, it's about losing. But *know* is the kinder word, and as long as we still have the luxury of choosing our words I can't begrudge you for going with something soft.

I shrug. "Not really."

I have a box beneath my bed. Full of poems she wrote me in shaky cursive. Now I don't have to wonder when she'll send me another.

"Just customers." I get a rag to clean the counter that doesn't need it. "Not sure what that says about me."

"Probably for the best." You sip your coffee.

We both stare out the main window, watching a perfect autumn afternoon pass with no poets to describe it. People are afraid now. Of the temperate cloudless days and the bright ominous stars. Beautiful things lurking around every corner. God forbid the sky turn some wonderful color for a fleeting moment and we find ourselves wanting to describe it. I don't know what we'd do. No one even posts on social media anymore. People panic that anything they write might be misconstrued as poetry. Looking over their shoulder for stray dactyls in dark alleys. Suddenly all experts in iambic pentameter and how to avoid it. A cold chill goes through the room anytime anything rhymes. People started burning diaries. I took to writing even my to-do lists on graph paper. Just to be safe.

"I was working," I confess this to you because that's the point of being a barista: you sometimes tell strangers your secrets. "Here. When it happened."

Just a few hours shy of the end of my shift. The world whimpering with no end. Curse him, T.S. Eliot, the lying bastard. Really it was only about half a day of real panic before people started putting the pieces together. It didn't take a genius to see the pattern, and it's not like the mathematicians were in any danger. The most infamous death was some brokerage firm CEO: there's still debate on whether or not he was murdered. Maybe it was an ill-timed heart attack. Or maybe, least likely of all, he really was a secret poet. All told, the number of casualties was barely a blip. Most families had at least one weird cousin to mourn, but it's not like all the D-1 athletes or wine-enthusiasts died. Some places were barely disturbed.

The schools, though, had already finished their poetry unit for the year. There were conferences that got completely eradicated. The open mics left decimated and dead quiet. Entire floors of psychiatric care facilities suddenly empty. All the writing retreats and home office nooks and local libraries. It took months to discover all the bodies. It took every living laureate. Not even the amateurs were spared. The youngest confirmed casualty was seven years old.

At the café it was my boss's boss who called to check in. He'd been getting nothing but dial tones and his relief was obvious when finally, somebody picked up. The shock in his tone, upon finding out it was me, was so upsetting that I hung up on him. I can't get through a closing shift now without seeing the tables filled with exquisite corpses. And all I have to cope is a notebook full of graph paper.

"It's how we lost my father," you say, because part of the reason people buy coffee from baristas is to sometimes tell them secrets. "We had no idea. Never suspected he was…" you gesture, some half-hearted wave of your fingers.

"I mean, *my dad,* of all people."

"I'm sorry to hear that." What else is there to say? All the creative condolers are dead themselves. Not to discount the few brave souls who started writing poetry again. They're new and it shows, but they are still alive. Maybe the rest of the poets are up in Poet Heaven, tinkering with little couplets and smiling down on them.

"I heard the funerals are awful." I imagine every ceremony is just forty-five minutes of everyone looking at each other, reiterating that they just don't know what to say. Each one more prosaic than the last.

"Terrible!" You laugh, and maybe it's on the edge of tears and maybe it isn't. "Absolutely terrible. To be honest the worst part is that they're just fucking *boring.*"

I wonder what they read at her funeral. Maybe just bible verses.

NOTES

Work Cited in "Survival Exhibit 54,550,001: NPO"

UVA Health. "NPO, or Nothing by Mouth: 3 Things You Need to Know." *UVA Radiology and Medical Imaging Blog for Patients*, 24 June 2022, https://blog.radiology.virginia.edu/npo-definition/.

Works Cited in "Survival Exhibit 270: Compression Artifact"

Clasen-Kelly, Fred. "A Mom Owed Nearly $102,000 for Her Son's Stay in a State Mental Health Hospital." *GBH*, 19 July 2023, https://www.wgbh.org/news/national/2023-07-19/a-mom-owed-nearly-102-000-for-her-sons-stay-in-a-state-mental-health-hospital.

Dalio, Ray. "Why the World Is on the Brink of Great Disorder." *TIME*, 26 June 2023, https://time.com/6286449/ray-dalio-world-great-disorder/.

Designer Soapbox. *HOW To Get APPROVED For $5,000 P*NDEMIC Loan After BEING DENIED... 🤑 [YOU MUST WATCH THIS!]*. 2020. *YouTube*, https://www.youtube.com/watch?v=_77WptBSEII.

DUPRÉ, Maggie Harrison. "AI Tasked With Destroying Humanity Now Trying New Tactic." *Futurism*, 15 Apr. 2023, https://futurism.com/ai-destroying-humanity-new-tactic.

Keith, Tamara. "When Politicians Have No Shame, the Old Rules Don't Apply." *NPR*, 15 Feb. 2023. *NPR*, https://www.npr.org/2023/02/15/1157049312/george-santos-politics-of-shame.

McCarthy, Daniel. "This July 4, Today's Youth Are Unprepared to Win a Revolutionary War." *New York Post*, 3 July 2023, https://nypost.com/2023/07/03/this-july-4-todays-youth-are-unprepared-to-win-a-revolutionary-war/.

Rahman, Khaleda. "Close-up Video Shows Texas Floating Barrier Has Circular Saws." *Newsweek*, 9 Aug. 2023, https://www.newsweek.com/video-texas-floating-barrier-saws-rio-grande-1818433.

Stone, Lillian. "Don't Buy Evil Chocolate." *The Takeout*, 15 June 2022, https://www.thetakeout.com/don-t-buy-evil-chocolate-1849065847/.

Villareal, Pristine. "Food Is Getting Cheaper. But Not for You." *NBC Palm Springs*, 9 Mar. 2023, https://nbcpalmsprings.com/2023/03/08/food-is-getting-cheaper-but-not-for-you/.

Wolf, Zachary B. "Analysis: The End of the World Order as We Know It | CNN Politics." *CNN*, 25 Jan. 2022, https://www.cnn.com/2022/01/25/politics/biden-us-foreign-affairs-what-matters/index.html.

"Survival Exhibit 5150: Grace Period Not Covered"

"I am having a cry in the doctor's office stairwell" is after the series "Having A Cry" by Becca Downs.

Additional References

Charles, Jos. *feeld*. Milkweed Editions, 2018.

Heit, Stephanie. *Psych Murders*. Wayne State Univ Press, 2022.

Heit, Stephanie. The Color She Gave Gravity. Operating System Press, 2017.

Hilborn, Neil. *The Future*. Button Poetry, 2024.

Machado, Carmen Maria. *Her Body and Other Parties: Stories*. Graywolf Press, 2017.

Machado, Carmen Maria. *In the Dream House*. Serpent's Tail, 2020.

Tate, James. *Hell, I Love Everybody.* Carcanet Poetry, 2023.

Vuong, Ocean. On Earth We're Briefly Gorgeous: A Novel. Penguin Books, 2021.

ACKNOWLEDGEMENTS

Immense gratitude and love to the following journals, which first published these poems:

Beyond the Veil – "Ode to My Big Dumb Gay Heart," "Upon My Passing," "Survival Exhibit 14: I say I Love You on the First Date," and "Survival Exhibit 470: Poem About Nature That is Also About Being Trans."

Twenty Bellows – "Wish Fulfillment Center"

I'd also like to thank the Mile High MFA program of Regis University. I received invaluable guidance and support there from fellow writers, mentors, and workshop leaders. Special thanks to Andrea Rexilius, Eric Baus, Erika T. Wurth, Mathias Svalina, Khadijah Queen, Carolina Ebeid, and Suzi Q. Smith. I am grateful for my poetry cohort and their undying creativity and cheerleading: this would not be the same without them. Special thanks to Anna Knapp for handling the works cited, and to Kathryn Richards for beta reading: I owe you both so much. Eternal love and gratitude to Maple Scoresby, for supporting me with good music, good times, and much needed humor. Thank you to the community of Denver writers I have encountered through various open-mic events. And my undying gratitude to the Mutiny Info Café for hosting their "Snap Crackle Poetry" monthly event and inviting me as a featured poet in June 2024. Thank you to the Girl-Dinner Poetry Collective, my work and life are both much richer, fuller, and more fun because of them. And to the wonderful weirdos of the world, I see you—may we all, every single day, get to be just a little bit weirder.

ABOUT THE AUTHOR

Megan Foley—aka: Cool Boots—is a queer poet, author, and artist who specializes in crying & trying. They write sad poems, they make unhinged art, and they spend 60% of their time on Thesaurus.com trying to find the exact word they want. Megan is a professional weirdo, a career cryptid, and the leading expert on how to make the world a weirder place.

ABOUT THE PRESS

South Broadway Press
is a publisher of poetry through books,
print journals, and on our online journal.

OUR MISSION

Our mission is to provide a platform through poetry, writing, and the arts for ideas that provide alternatives to the harmful systems and ideologies that we historically have and continue to live among. We are interested in work that points us towards symbiosis with not just other humans, but with all beings in this moment, all beings past, and those future beings that will be impacted by the choices we collectively, and individually, make today. We focus our attention on love as a guiding force. Not a love that only reactively supports those who have been afflicted by oppression, but a love that is willing to disrupt, disobey, and proactively prevent and redirect the potential forthcoming affliction around us. A love that is resolute in its boundaries for itself and others. A love that takes the form of dissent, resistance, and in the words of John Lewis, a love that is willing to "get into good trouble".

www.southbroadwaypress.org

OUR SEAL

Our seal is **the Bear, the Wrench, and the Quill.**

The Bear as a symbol of balancing softness with strength. The Bear as a call to approaching the caves of our internal worlds with curiosity. To slow living, and to laying witness to ourselves as not just material beings walking this Earth, but celestial beings, such as the great bear that graces the winter sky above us.

The Wrench as a symbol of disruption. A willingness to throw a wrench into the gears of fascism.

The Quill as a reminder of the adage that "the pen is mightier than the sword", and a calling to approach our work and play with that integrity and power in mind.

Our seal is also a nod to **Mutiny Information Cafe**, a bookstore, coffee shop, and community hub for over ten years now. A space that has time and again proved home for the cultivation of revolutionary ideas and the soft hearts that hold them.

www.ingramcontent.com/pod-product-compliance
Lightning Source LLC
LaVergne TN
LVHW091006080826
845145LV00003B/1153

* 9 7 8 1 7 3 5 0 3 5 5 7 4 *